10 PRINCIPLES OF A CHARACTER COACH

"Working with Coach Waters was truly one of the highlights of my administrative career. The opportunity to witness his value-based approach to developing young men through the sport of basketball was inspiring and the key ingredient in his successful career. Leading with integrity never goes out of style. This book is a must read for anyone in a leadership position."

—**Lee Reed**, Athletic Director, Georgetown University

"There is no more important responsibility for coaches than teaching their players to become future leaders in life! Winning has its place. So, too does teaching teamwork and individual fundamentals.

Coaching is so much more! Gary Waters has provided in his book an important reminder. More than a reminder, however, it is a roadmap for coaches to encourage their players to exhibit the qualities of character that do inspire others to exhibit similar qualities in their lives.

Equally important, Waters' book leads us to self-examination of our own values and champions character development of us as coaches as well. This is a book that will make an impact on all who read it!"

—**Jim Haney**, Executive Director,
National Association of Basketball Coaches (NABC)

"Legendary Coach John Wooden said, "Never mistake activity for achievement." Like the increasingly fast-paced game of basketball, our world is stuffed full of activity… often forged at the expense of deeper, lasting achievement.

We move too fast for our own good. Playing life with pace and space needs a NorthStar to ensure that high purpose and true achievement don't get sideline along the way… Coach Waters calls a valuable timeout to help connect us to 'playbook' principle that score anywhere in the game of life. He understands both victory and beyond competition… how to get both. I believe personal wins await as you join him. So, lace up your mind and heart, run through this book, and play ball with character and deeper confidence! Thanks, Gary, for coaching us once again!"

—Morris (Coach Mo) Michalski,
Basketball Specialist/Director, Athletes in Action (AIA)

"Gary has written a must-read that transcends any professional genre. The *10 Principles of a Character Coach* establishes character and morality-driven fundamental practices, for all aspiring and veteran coaches to infuse, into their coaching DNA. This book is a blueprint for individuals, who aspire to lead others."

—Mike Krzyzewski, Hall of Fame Inductee,
Head Basketball Coach, Duke University

"In a world where values seem to be decreasing and tweets are increasing, the standards by which we measure a person's character has become blurred. Gary Waters *10 Principles of a Character Coach* reminds us what is important and how to conduct our lives to make a difference, in the lives of others. This book guides us through Waters' life experiences as a coach, father and man of God, sharing golden nuggets of wisdom on character building."

—**Bill Self**, Hall of Fame Inductee,
Head Basketball Coach, University of Kansas

"Today every coach wants to win and play at a high level. Coach Waters, *Ten Principles of a Character Coach* is a must read that will help coaches not only win games, but develop the next generation of leaders. He is giving us tools to leave a legacy!"

—**Tommy Kyle**, Executive Director, Nations of
Coaches

"Having competed against Gary's teams in the Big East Conference, I always admired how prepared and disciplined they were. After reading *10 Principles of a Character Coach* I have a better understanding of why that was so. Coach Waters understandings the value of high-quality people of character. It's a simple but vital part of any group's success and in *10 Principles of a Character Coach* the reader will gain insight into the qualities that can help any group or individual reach their full potential."

—**Jay Wright**, Head Basketball Coach,
Villanova University

"Gary Waters is a true professional in the coaching ranks. His basketball knowledge is outstanding, but his ability and desire to invest in the character development of his players and staff was a driving force of his success. In his book, *Ten Principles of a Character Coach*, he shares the principles and applicable practices one needs to develop a culture in your profession that instills integrity to those you serve."

—**Mike Anderson**, Head Basketball Coach,
St. John's University

"In *10 Principles of a Character Coach*, Gary Waters is calling us to examine how we interact and impact those around us. He shares with us those character traits that will help us influence those we lead and contribute to the development of their character. *10 Principles of a Character Coach*, is a must read for those who are presently in or entering the coaching profession, whether it is business or in the area of athletics."

—**Tubby Smith**, Head Basketball Coach,
High Point University

"In my 48 years of coaching, Basketball has always been a vehicle to develop the next generation. The life lessons learned in athletics are instrumental in the growth of the student-athlete. The *Character Coach* epitomizes the foundational truths of integrity, discipline and character."

—**Vivian Stringer**, Hall of Fame Inductee,
Head Basketball Coach, Rutgers University

"With the ever-evolving dynamics in any professional genre, there remains one constant for all leadership success; CHARACTER. Gary Waters has done a tremendous job of conveying practical character attributes, for leadership development. The *Ten Principles of a Character Coach* is a must read for all professionals."

—Tom Izzo, Hall of Fame Inductee,
Head Basketball Coach, Michigan State University

10
PRINCIPLES OF
A CHARACTER
COACH

COACH GARY WATERS

NEW YORK

LONDON • NASHVILLE • MELBOURNE • VANCOUVER

10 PRINCIPLES OF A CHARACTER COACH

© 2021 **COACH GARY WATERS**

Published in New York, New York, by Morgan James Publishing. Morgan James is a trademark of Morgan James, LLC. www.MorganJamesPublishing.com

Scripture quotations taken from The Holy Bible, New International Version® NIV® Copyright © 1973, 1978, 1984, 2011 by Biblica, Inc.™ Used by permission of Zondervan. All rights reserved worldwide. www.zondervan.com

ISBN 978-1-63195-086-5 eBook
ISBN 978-1-63195-085-8 case laminate
Library of Congress Control Number: 2020904132

Front cover image courtesy Cleveland State University (Sports Information Department).

Cover Design by:
Rachel Lopez
www.r2cdesign.com

Morgan James is a proud partner of Habitat for Humanity Peninsula and Greater Williamsburg. Partners in building since 2006.

Get involved today! Visit
www.MorganJamesBuilds.com

TABLE OF CONTENTS

FOREWORD

by **Larry DeSimpelare**
Commissioner of the Crossroad Conference (NAIA)

It was February 28, 1998 and the Kent State Flashes were about to play an undefeated Akron team in the first round of the MAC post season tournament. Gary Waters was in his second year as the head coach of the Golden Flashes and this game would become the "beginning" of some amazing and unprecedented success for Kent State Basketball.

The Akron Zips were undefeated in conference play this season, led by a lethal combination of guards. A lightning quick and explosive point guard, and a tough, gritty and talented scoring guard. The previous two match-ups in this rivalry were not even close. Akron had beaten us on our home court by 25 early in January, and just 9 days earlier by 17 at the JAR (James A Rhodes Arena).

This Kent State team only won 13 games that season, but were beginning to show signs of competitiveness. This game would be a breakthrough performance that would set the stage for years of championships and unprecedented success.

The game wasn't really as close as the score indicated. Kent dominated from the tip. It was a fast paced, high scoring affair. Akron was a physically tough and talented team, and they would not back down. The game was physical, and personal as most rival games are.

In the aftermath of our celebration, and the joyous 15-minute bus ride home, we were met with a barrage of phone calls demanding that our star player be "suspended" for his actions in the game. One of the best players on our team, and in the league had set a physical screen during the late stages of the game. The play happened so fast that neither team noticed, nor did any official. No foul was called.

Upon review of the play, it was obvious that the screen was illegal. Borderline dirty. We prided ourselves on toughness, competitiveness and a desire to out-work our opponent. But Gary was committed to teaching our players greater lessons than those of the game. This would be a defining moment in this CHARACTER COACH's Journey!

The next day, the commissioner of our league called and told Gary that although the play was physical and borderline "dirty", he was not going to suspend our player. After carefully reviewing the play, he could not determine the intent and did not want to hurt our chances in the next round. I can remember overhearing the Gary's part of the conversation with our commissioner, and after hanging up the phone, Coach Waters had summoned me to get our player in his office.

When our player arrived, our entire staff was called into the office to be a part of the conversation. My first thought was of Gary simply punishing our player verbally, or maybe he would have one of us "run" him for the behavior. That would not be the case. Gary sat with his player as a father would after a son who just walked away from his first car accident. He dug deep into the young man, and probed his heart. He took the time to truly asses the intent, the act and process behind the action. There were tears by both player and coach. It was a very real and poignant moment for a young coach. As I look back on it today, Gary was using this opportunity to not only teach our player a valuable lesson, he was also teaching his young staff.

Gary did not need to talk to the commissioner to know if he would suspend our player, he knew what he needed to do from the first time he watched the tape. He also knew that he needed to connect with his player. He wanted the player to acknowledge and accept the behavior. He wanted to look into the eyes of his rising star and see if he had the character that would be needed for what the future would hold. He found his answer. You can look in the record book to see just how successful this group became. Most will say it is because of the talent. Don't get me wrong, you need to have talent to win like we did at Kent State. But this book will give you a much DEEPER look at the real reasons behind the success. Our player was suspended for the next game. We lost that game. Yet, this was way more about BUILDING CHARACTER and not just simply showing it. Our player led us to the first of many MAC Championships, along with setting the foundation for what would become an ELITE 8 team just a few years later. Gary wasn't just interested in being a CHARACTER COACH, he was interested in building a CHARACTER TEAM. Just a couple years earlier, I remember sitting with Gary in the lobby of Times Square in NYC. The final four was being held in New York, and Gary had recently been named the new coach at Kent. This was going to be the first "staff" meeting for myself, Kevin Heck and Garland Mance with our new coach. As we were waiting, I saw Tubby Smith (who was coaching at Georgia that year, and would win a national championship at Kentucky just a couple years later) approach Gary and say, "You can't take that job. You cannot win there!" Gary simply smiled and said…. "I appreciate it Tubby, but we will!" I wasn't sure if it was arrogance or supreme confidence, but I remember being juiced up to coach for this man. Little did I know how much my life would be affected by his influence. From Kent State to Rutgers, from Rutgers to Cleveland State; I have seen the consistency of a CHARACTER COACH and the impact it has had. It would be easy to only look at the victories on the court, and of course, there were many. The values of a CHARACTER COACH demonstrate success in the classroom as well, as every kid that played for Gary Waters for four years, or through their eligibility at Cleveland State earned their degree. Young men armed with a degree, confidence and work ethic to take on the world. They are also armed with the intangibles of being coached by someone who instilled these strong values inside this book.

These CHARACTER COACH VALUES are time tested and true. You should also know that being a CHARACTER COACH means you will be tested. Your commitment to being a CHARACTER COACH will not always be easy. The temptations to cut corners, look the other way, or even blatantly choose the wrong option, all for the desire of the win will present itself more often than you can imagine. Winning was never the purpose of this CHARACTER COACH, but always the goal! Make the culture your purpose, and the victories will be often and sometimes overwhelming! I truly hope you have a pen or highlighter with you when you read this book. You will want to mark things down, underline important parts, and highlight things throughout the book. It is a great reference and reminder of how CHARACTER is the viable piece in developing success.

I think our world sometimes view character as something of convenience. Simply put, Character of convenience is not character...in fact, it might be the exact opposite. Character shows up when you need it the most, and if you feel you have to justify your character—you probably missed it.

I am a better father because of Gary Waters. I am a better husband because of Gary Waters. I am a better friend because of Gary Waters. And most importantly, I am a better FAITHFUL leader because of Gary Waters.

I had the benefit of nearly 25 years together. You have the benefit of those lessons being condensed into one book. Read it with a focus and purpose that Coach would demand if you we're lacing them up for him. You will be glad you did!

INTRODUCTION

I woke up one morning in the fall of 2009 and sat on the side of my bed, mulling over a conversation I had with two coaches the previous night about the state of college basketball.

Enough is enough, I thought.

Dr. James Naismith The Inventor of Basketball (Courtesy of Escuela Virtual de Deportes-Coldeportes.)

It was time to bring back to coaching what Dr. Naismith intended when he created the sport.

"Naismith believed that if you elected to be a coach, it was also your responsibility to be an advisor, counselor, and father figure, and to act at all times as an example to the athletes in your care."[1]

He also envisioned that sports should "develop character, foster patriotism, and instill ethical values that would serve participants well in later life."[2]

These principles are more important than the game itself and therefore, should be important to every coach.

But today, coaches place less value on the integrity-based principles of leadership, and have instead prioritized accolades, prominence, and financial gain.

I started to witness the rapid deterioration of principle-driven coaching during my third and fourth years at Cleveland State, although the gradual decline was evident to me years earlier when I coached at Rutgers University. The difference at Rutgers, however, was at that time, in that part of the country, respect for coaching and coaches was still prominent in the profession.

I was in my third year at Cleveland State in 2009. We had just completed a championship season and NCAA tournament appearance.

---

1   Milton S. Katz, P. B., & Naismith, I. (2007). *Breaking Through: John B. McClendon, Basketball Legend and Civil Rights Pioneer.* Fayetteville: University of Arkansas Press. (15)

2   Ibid, 14.

2009 Cleveland State Championship Team
(Courtesy of Cleveland State University)

We beat Wake Forest in the first round of the regional finals. In a later round, we lost to the University of Arizona in a close game. As a result, we were recognized as a mid-major power for the upcoming season.

The success we had the previous season prompted us to use an alternative recruiting strategy for the upcoming season—we decided to go after top-tier athletes. The types of schools recruiting these players were often of a much higher-profile and could offer different incentives and perks than we could.

I realized quickly during this process that for some coaches, and some players, character and morality were an afterthought, and that realization—the decline of core values—was the catalyst for writing this book. My hope is that my explanation of tested and proven character principles will help coaches understand the significance of running their programs with character and integrity.

Beyond coaches, this book is useful for parents and student-athletes, who can use the principles as benchmarks to identify the type of coach and behavior they want to be associated with. Marginally, this book is also for leaders, managers, and all manner of professionals, as the ideas and values I discuss are readily applicable to any field.

Coaches today have been inundated with so much information that comparatively, they are just as overwhelmed with data and messaging as the children of this Information Age. This generation is hearing, seeing, and experiencing much more than previous generations. Character examples are needed now, more than ever.

The value structure has changed drastically within our society today. Behaviors and attitudes which would have been frowned upon in previous decades are widely accepted today, and this shift has indubitably impacted the coaching culture, especially in terms of values and the moral compass of the profession.

While these character principles are important to coaches at any level, they are equally as important to parents and their children. I believe following these principles will not only make you a better person, but also enhance your ability to train and lead as a coach.

The ten character principles I discuss in this book are:

Principle 1: God Over Everything
Principle 2: Improve Yourself, And Others

Principle 3: Live with Integrity and Honesty

Principle 4: Treat Others the Way You Want to Be Treated

Principle 5: Love Unconditionally

Principle 6: Work Hard at What Matters

Principle 7: Value and Demonstrate Loyalty

Principle 8: Empower and Serve your Staff

Principle 9: Honor the Profession and the Players

Principle 10: Leave a Character Legacy

I believe that coaching is a gift given to those who can touch lives in a positive manner. It is the coach's responsibility to improve each player's quality of life through their association with the sport.

I believe that coaching is a gift given to those who can touch lives in a positive manner.

How coaches demonstrate this modus operandi is important to each player's value structure. A coach can have a positive impact on a player's life if he exemplifies and elevates integrity as the norm, and is both vocal and visible about the need for it. In fact, I believe coaches should advocate for values just as strongly as they do physical fitness.

Coaches should have a daily practice of checking in with themselves in service of the profession, to always be aware of their conduct, and consistently seeking ways in which they can enrich their personal lives and those around them.

Let's venture into a life of coaching driven by character principles.

PRINCIPLE 1
GOD OVER EVERYTHING

Put God First in Everything You Do

It was my fourth year at Cleveland State, and things were on track for another interesting and successful year. The morning of my first day entering the new season, I went to my prayer and meditation room for my private time with my Lord and Savior Jesus Christ, a discipline that has been a part of my everyday routine for most of my adult life. I completed my reading for the day, as each morning I spent time reviewing the Scriptures for spiritual nourishment and wisdom, and then I thanked God for everything He had done, as well as those things He had yet to do.

Each day when I would arrive at work, I would gather my coaches to pray. As a staff, it was important to us that we put God first.

2008-09 Cleveland State Basketball Staff (Courtesy of Cleveland State University)

We would have our prayer time before we would discuss any office or basketball matters. We knew that our focus on faith was key to our success on the court.

I believe when God is at the forefront of everything you do as opposed to self, it puts your day into perspective.

I believe when God is at the forefront of everything you do as opposed to self, it helps you to visualize what you want to accomplish during the day, adding perspective, providing the *why* for what you've visualized. Throughout the years, I have found that this simple practice of visualizing the outcome also leads to completion.

After our prayer time and staff discussions, we met with each team member at breakfast to make sure they were going to class and honoring their responsibilities. By holding them accountable, our staff was able to pour into each player and guide them on the right path. We followed this schedule each day.

We were preparing for a season with many new faces after having a successful season the previous year. I could see the potential in this group, even though we had lost some important pieces from the championship team.

Over the course of the 2009 championship season, we had many experiences which typified the concept of having God at the front of what we did as a team.

One Friday that November during preseason, we traveled to Michigan to scrimmage Eastern Michigan University. Our scrimmage game wasn't till Saturday morning and since we arrived early enough on Friday, we decided to attend a special

2009 Horizon League Championship Team
(Courtesy of Cleveland State University)

musical event performed by the famous gospel singers the Winans, at Perfecting Church in Detroit.

This experience marked the first thing we did together as a team independent of basketball, and for me, it signified that God would be at the forefront of our program. We dedicated our season with this mission in mind.

That night, a special moment of commitment occurred in front of the congregation. After the musical ended, Pastor Winans prayed for our team. In my mind and heart, I knew this moment was providential, because Perfecting Church was affiliated with the University of Detroit-Mercy, one of our conference rivals.

The recruiting class that year consisted of many junior college transfers already set in their ways, many of which weren't necessarily positive or constructive.

Establishing and modeling character principles would be important to setting a foundation for them to follow and for their future. My top assistant coach at the time was Jayson Gee, whose recruiting prowess was well-known at the collegiate level, and who I personally considered to be one of the top assistant coaches in the country. Jayson's job was to make sure our current recruiting class embraced and exemplified our character-driven culture. Our responsibility overall was to get everyone on board, from the players to the coaches, but especially the new recruits.

The players who remained from the championship team were led by a person of character, Norris Cole, a two-time

NBA champion with LeBron James during the Miami Heat run. Norris is truly a person of notable character and was an exemplary force in building the team.

He and the remaining players already understood our culture, so for them, putting God first was the norm. The incoming players were aware during the recruiting process of

Norris Cole Coached by Coach Waters (Courtesy of Cleveland State University)

our way of doing things, so putting God first became part of their mindset as well.

Year four had its difficulties, starting with a trip to Cancun, Mexico, where we played the likes of the University of Kentucky and the University of Virginia. When we returned from Cancun, we played the University of West Virginia in front of a capacity crowd. These teams were all highly ranked and would eventually be NCAA Tournament participants. We prayed as a team before each contest, acknowledging our reliance on God and asking Him for the physical and mental strength to do our best.

The conference season was challenging at the start, primarily due to the inexperience and youth of our group.

We had lost five seniors to graduation the previous year, who all played substantial minutes and provided outstanding leadership.

Despite our early challenges, as the season progressed, we became better acquainted as a unit, realizing that to achieve the success we were expecting and praying for, we'd need to get serious about putting and keeping God first. The more we incorporated this belief as individuals and as a team, the more competitive we became in our conference.

When you put yourself first, neglecting or ignoring God's providence and power, you tend to become prideful, self-centered, and over-ambitious. These personality traits run counter to character-driven values and a team-centric philosophy.

By acknowledging God first, recognizing Him as our Source, we remained grounded. We worked hard, but we credited every accomplishment to God, not just our own personal talents. The same was true of the previous season. It wasn't just our skills or talents that made us champions—it was God's faithfulness. We put the Lord first throughout that year and the joy we experienced from each accomplishment was much more rewarding than it was when we believed it was only about ourselves.

The fourth year saddled us with many challenges, and we went through a great deal of turmoil, but with God leading the way, our difficulties were more meaningful. We viewed our circumstances within the larger framework of our faith.

Perhaps the most telling experience of our God-first mentality was when we played for the conference championship at Butler University the year before. This was the same Butler University that went on to play for the NCAA national championship the following year, and the year after that.

Playing on Butler's home court (the same court where the movie *Hoosiers* was filmed) put us at a distinct disadvantage, and we needed an extra push. I believed then as I do now that God can accomplish extraordinary things with ordinary people. Our situation was nothing uncommon to the One we had put first in our lives.

That night, I used a story from the Bible, Joshua 6:1-27, to inspire us and give us strength. In the story, at the Lord's command, Joshua, seven priests, and several other guards carried a sacred chest called the Ark of the Covenant around the walls of Jericho once a day for six straight days. On the seventh day, they were instructed to march around the town seven times, and while the priests blew their trumpets, everyone was to yell as loud as they could.

Everyone does as they're told, and on the seventh day, as the trumpets sounded and they bellowed as loud as they could, the walls came crashing down.

Before the game in the basement of Hinkle Fieldhouse, we orchestrated a similar strategy to accomplish our mission. We marched around the basement carrying an ark we constructed, blew through horns we created, and yelled at

Cleveland State vs Butler HL Championship Game
(Courtesy of Cleveland State University)

the top of our lungs. We were so loud that a bewildered bunch of venue security guards rushed down the stairs to see what was going on.

More than anything, our modern-day Jericho demonstration was a declaration that God was at the head of our program. We accomplished the unexpected that night by defeating Butler University on their court, one of the most difficult places to win. God honored us by reciprocating our efforts with a victory.

That night, an ordinary group of men accomplished an extraordinary feat and received their first NCAA Tournament bid. So, even though year four was nothing like our championship year, with God at the helm, we had some success and looked forward to the promise of our future.

I share these experiences to encourage you to let God be your guide as you carry out the principles of being a character-driven coach. There's a scripture that exemplifies this concept that you'd be well served to adopt as a part of your team or family ethos: "Trust in the Lord with all your heart, and lean not on your own understanding; and in all your ways acknowledge Him, and He will direct your path." (Proverbs 3:5-6, NKJV)

PRINCIPLE 2
IMPROVE YOURSELF AND OTHERS

Be true to yourself, help others, make each day
your masterpiece, make friendship a fine art, drink
deeply from good books—especially the Bible,
build a shelter against a rainy day, give thanks for
your blessings and pray for guidance every day.
—**John Wooden**, Famous UCLA Coach,
Winner of (10) NCAA National Championships

During my coaching career, I started each day with the idea in mind that I would do whatever I could to make myself and those around me better.

One way I did this with my staff was by seeking out and providing professional opportunities for them to enhance

Jermaine Kimbrough Assistant Basketball Coach (Courtesy of Cleveland State University)

their knowledge and education. For example, I gave one of my coaches, Jermaine Kimbrough, a homegrown Clevelander, the time and flexibility he needed to complete his master's degree during his first two years on the staff.

Jermaine wanted to further himself within the profession, and it would be to his advantage to have a higher education than the players he was working with.

As a staff, we were committed to spending numerous hours on professional development and training to increase our knowledge within the profession.

Our entire staff committed a considerable number of hours to professional development and training to learn more about coaching, training, and leadership. There is less emphasis on this aspect of career development today; nothing like the early days when it was required.

When I started in the profession, having a teaching certificate and undergraduate degree was a requirement.

I also had to earn a minor degree in coaching to help me better instruct and educate student-athletes. Today, the requirements are less stringent for a person wanting to coach, but the more knowledgeable you are in your chosen profession, the more valuable you will be to your vocation. King Solomon of the Old Testament said, "The fear of the Lord is the beginning of knowledge, but fools despise wisdom and instruction." (Proverbs 1:7, NIV)

At times, you will have to make tough choices for the benefit of your team and the individuals involved, but embrace this inevitability rather than avoid it, and you'll be much more prepared to make the right decision when you're faced with such choices. At the end of year four, I had my own choice to make.

As I mentioned earlier, we had brought in four junior-college transfers to help bolster our team with collegiate-level maturity and experience. This left our program with several underclassmen and a talented red-shirt transfer, Aaron Pogue.

Aaron was a teammate of Norris Cole at Dayton Dunbar High School in Ohio, and both were two-

Aaron Pogue drives against Ohio State (Courtesy of Cleveland State University)

time state champions during their time together at Dunbar. Aaron was also Third Team All-American during his senior year. Their familiarity on and off the court made them a formidable duo, a difficult combination for opponents to handle.

With four competitive junior college transfers, our team had seemingly unlimited potential. But we also had serious issues undermining our would-be successes that eventually became too conspicuous to ignore—questionable attitudes and challenges with their character.

Addressing these concerns became the focal point of our program for nearly the entire year. We spent a great deal of time working through character issues, and we did so at the expense of working on other aspects of making our team better. At the end of the season, I had to decide whether to keep the four junior college transfers for another year or help them find places that would better suit their ways of living.

A Lee Reed Athletic Director Cleveland State University (Courtesy of Cleveland State University)

So, before I made this difficult decision, I consulted with my athletic director, Lee Reed. Lee was the primary reason I decided to accept the head coaching position at

Cleveland State. He was truly a coaches' administrator, one that I could trust and I knew he had my back. Once we met, Lee told me he would be behind me regardless—whatever decision I would make. Lee is presently the athletic director at Georgetown University of the Big East Conference.

Why was this a difficult decision? Because I felt I could help them. I was certain I could turn them around. They competed hard for us when given the opportunity, but their adjustment to the college experience was at times problematic, and in the end, I chose to move each player on to another place. I felt it was a necessary change for them, their future, and our team.

Now, imagine losing four experienced, essential players at one time. Their transition created a void in our program and we had to work extremely hard to fill in the gap. But my goal from day one was to help each player become better every day, so regardless of the price we had to pay, it was worth it.

Ultimately, we replaced the junior-college transfers with three quality freshmen who helped us compete for three other conference championships.

The next year, our fifth season, turned out to be a special season. We won twenty-seven games, the most in program history. We also won the regular season conference championship. How did we accomplish this in the aftermath of such a major loss?

We made a commit-ment to becoming better individually and as a team each day. Norris Cole became the MVP of the conference that season, as well as defensive player of the year. This commendation was one no other player in the conference had ever received in the same season. He became better in every statistical category than he had been in previous seasons.

Norris had also committed to bringing someone with him whenever he worked out. When he entered our program his freshmen year, he befriended a teammate named J'Nathan Bullock, an all-conference player who was later signed by the New York Jets as an undrafted free agent.

J'Nathan Bullock competes against Wake Forest in NCAA Tournament (Courtesy of Cleveland State University)

J'Nathan worked on his skills every day, and shared Norris's commit-ment, so he and Norris worked out together and pushed each other regularly.

Norris made this same commitment his junior year to another player on the team. We employed this philosophy in our program throughout the years and by doing so, we created an environment where our players could cultivate their personal greatness and inspire another to reach theirs.

Norris and J'Nathan were so committed to this philosophy that even on game days when we were on the road, they would ask me to help them find a place where they could work on their game during the morning hours. This was the type of culture we had created at Cleveland State and everyone had bought into it to better themselves.

We lost in the conference tournament semi-finals to our nemesis, Butler University. Butler went on to play in the NCAA Final Four Tournament championship game. Since the Horizon League was a one-bid conference, the other teams only had secondary tournament options, which meant we had to settle for the National Invitational Tournament (NIT), the next best thing. We accepted the bid to play in the NIT, advanced to the regional finals, and lost to a good team, the College of Charleston, in a close match.

Our team and staff had bought into a system, a system that fostered rich opportunities for the mutual reinforcement of personal growth and collaborative connection. We vowed to uphold this practice of bettering ourselves and each other. The players embraced character, held themselves academically accountable, and put the work in to improve their on-court skills.

I'd like to leave you with one final thought on this matter, a memorable quote I discovered when doing the research for this work:

"Being inspired by others can be great to motivate you, but discovering your own reasons to progress and better yourself is what will keep you strong."

—Anonymous

PRINCIPLE 3
LIVE WITH INTEGRITY AND HONESTY

*Leaders must exemplify integrity and
earn the trust of their teams through their
everyday actions. When you do this, you
set high standards for everyone...And
when you do so with positive energy and
enthusiasm for shared goals and purpose,
you can deeply connect with your team...*

—**Marilyn Hewson**, Chairwoman, President, and CEO
Lockheed-Martin Manufacturing Company

Never recruit at any cost!

When I started in the profession, I heard this bit of advice perhaps more than any other. After all, recruiting is the lifeblood of college coaching. My takeaway? Recruit with integrity, because *how* you recruit and *who* you recruit will shape your team's culture.

In his book *Leading with Boundaries,* Dr. Henry Cloud says, "As a leader, you're always going to get a combination of two things: what you create and what you allow."

Treat your recruiting strategy and standards as circumspectly as anything you do, because ultimately, you are responsible for the foundational values embraced by those under your leadership.

Regardless of how talented a potential recruit was, I never crossed the line. My character and values prescribe my actions, and to engage players in a way that I knew was wrong would've been tantamount to personal failure.

I try to live by a rule that can be explained using the mathematical concept of congruency. To be congruent, two figures or objects must be consistent in size and shape. From an attitudinal standpoint, your behavior must be consistent with your goals. When you say you're going to do something, you've got to follow through and do it.

During my sixth year at Cleveland State, we signed four high-level recruits. Many scouting services ranked us among the top in mid-major recruiting, to the point where we were being measured against the top high-major programs in the country.

Two of the four recruits we signed were high-major prospects. Both relocated to high-major programs as fifth-year transfers. Anton Grady, from Cleveland, transferred to Wichita State and Ike Nwamu from Greensboro, North Carolina, transferred a second time to University of Nevada, Las Vegas.

Out of high school, Ike was a YouTube sensation, known for his high-flying dunks. This was right at the beginning of the transfer wave that was sweeping the country in Division I basketball. Over the next three years, we lost five players to high-major programs.

This recruiting trend continued to tick upward year after year, spreading throughout Division I like a virus at pandemic levels. But the big question is, *was this recruiting being done ethically?* Only the coaches and programs involved can answer sincerely.

Spencer Johnson, a renowned American physician and author once said, "Integrity is telling myself the truth and honesty is telling the truth to others."

To think in terms of integrity and honesty, you have to reach down into your inner sanctum, the place where your core values are processed and where you distinguish between right and wrong.

Integrity and honesty are character traits all coaches need to have to be true to themselves and anyone they associate with. We'd all be well served to adopt the paradigm of Marcus Aurelius, a Roman emperor who ruled from 161 to 180 AD, who said, "If it is not right do not do it; if it is not true do not say it."

At the beginning of the year during the recruiting period, my staff and I were confronted with a negative recruiting situation. One of our league competitors was recruiting the same prospect we were. Each program was always trying to get a leg up in the arms war of recruiting.

The recruit in question visited the opposition's school first and was scheduled to visit our campus later in the week. During his forty-eight hours with the opposing school, their recruiting staff bad-mouthed our program with negative and false propaganda. By the time the recruit reached our school, he was all but convinced that we weren't right for him.

When he told us all the opposing school had said, my staff was furious and thought about retaliation. But I would have none of it. We would not respond in-kind, no matter how angry we were or how wrong they were. Inadvertently so, the opposing school had given us an opportunity to demonstrate the integrity we preached about.

Instead of striking back, we spoke highly of their program and refrained from discussing the negative comments any further during his visit. We showed him "The Waters Way" of doing things.

"The Waters Way" was a creed I drafted that our coaches and players pledged to model. This creed represented everything we stood for and aimed to exemplify us as individuals of character and integrity.

"The Waters Way" Program Creed

Our approach—one that involved us taking the high road by refusing to slander the school that had slandered us—worked so well that the recruit wanted to commit on the spot, before even consulting with his parents.

We convinced him to go back home and talk it over with them, however, because we didn't want him to make a hasty decision and thought it best that he have his parents' guidance. This also gave us the ability to control the first right of refusal.

Ultimately, we decided to go in a different direction, concluding that our program wasn't a good fit for him. The big point here, however, is that even though we were offended by the opposition's tactics in the defamation of our program, we would not compromise our integrity by stooping to such a low level.

But what surprised me most about the entire situation was the opposing coaches' mindset. They saw slandering us

DeAndre Brown going up against Loyola of Chicago (Courtesy of Cleveland State University)

as nothing more than a means to an end. They didn't see it as wrong. In terms of character, clearly, our profession needed an overhaul.

DeAndre Brown, a three-year starter in his fifth year off a medical red-shirt, would lead our team at the start of our sixth season. He had a strong supporting cast with four other starters from the previous year who understood our culture and who, like DeAndre, had also developed into character exemplars.

We encouraged our starters to lead the rest of the pack, especially the talented new players, down the path of integrity and honesty. We pressed into them our chosen definition of integrity, "Always do what's right, even when no one is watching."

"Always do what's right, even when no one is watching."

Oprah says it this way, "Real integrity is doing the right thing, knowing that nobody's going to know whether you did it or not."

In the locker room, honesty and integrity were the linchpins of our camaraderie. Without these traits, there is no way we could have coexisted as a family.

Outsiders may think the locker room is a place where players disrespect each other, saying and doing whatever they feel without filter. But it's the complete opposite when the coaching staff insists on courtesy, empathy, and respect for others.

The players might kid around, tell jokes, or prank each other, but when they do, it's all in good-natured fun. Disrespect and disparaging discourse are not tolerated in character-driven locker rooms.

On the other hand, locker rooms are an open environment, the place where players and coaches retreat immediately after emotional wins and losses, to celebrate victories or release frustration. And, because of the candid nature of locker room settings, personality types, traits, and differences are often on full display—occasional outbursts should be expected.

Locker room conditions revolve around trust. At Cleveland State, we were confident in our "what's said in the locker room, stays in the locker room" credo—we had faith in each other and didn't have to worry about duplicity.

We had lost Norris that year, who had been the glue of our unit, but as we progressed, I believed we could have an outstanding season. Three of the four returning starters, Aaron Pogue, Trey Harmon, and Jeremy Montgomery had played together for three years. The fourth starter, Tim Kamczyc, was a two-year starter at his position. Once DeAndre Brown returned to the mix, his three-year-starting experience solidified the unit.

We were excited about the potential of this group, not to mention the outstanding recruiting class we had assembled. Our excitement only grew when we won an early contest at Vanderbilt University, who was ranked sixth in the country in the SEC. We handled them easily on their home court, each player on our roster showing incredible promise.

Reflecting on my eleven years at Cleveland State, this may have been the best team we assembled. What's most remarkable about that year is how each player handled himself throughout the year, showing examples of integrity and honesty as pillars of their character.

Coach Waters during the NIT Competition (Courtesy of Cleveland State University)

The year ended with a tough loss in the Horizon League Tournament Semifinals, and an NIT defeat at Stanford University of the PAC Ten Conference.

(Stanford eventually won the NIT Championship that season).

After they won the tournament, I talked with Johnny Dawkins, their head coach.

He commented, "You guys were the toughest team we've played in this tournament." Johnny Dawkins was an All-American at Duke University, and he led Coach Mike Krzyzewski's team to his first NCAA National Championship.

We started and ended the season with integrity and honesty as staples of our system, allowing us to close the books on another stellar, successful year, with all four seniors graduating.

Charles F. Glassman, M.D. and author says, "Some say if you want success, surround yourself with successful people. I say, if you want true and lasting success, surround yourself with people of integrity."

I'm with Dr. Glassman. Coaches of character live by the belief that integrity and honesty are ingrained in the framework of who they are. Epitomize these values and you'll create a culture where trust and honor form the peak of your belief system—two things it's hard to win without.

TREAT OTHERS THE WAY YOU WANT TO BE TREATED

*Respect for ourselves guides our manners,
respect for others guides our manners.*
—Laurence Sterne, Irish Novelist,
English Writer, Anglican Clergyman

I t's called The Golden Rule for good reason: it has immense value and this simple maxim, derived from Scripture, is heralded as the gold standard of all other rules for relationships and social interaction.

I'm sure you've heard numerous iterations of it. The biblical version says, "Do unto others as you would have them do unto you." In philosophical circles, it's referred to as an ethic of reciprocity.

As a principle here it is: Treat others the way you want to be treated. Another way of saying it is to treat others with respect.

Respect, at the most basic level, is simply the courteous treatment of others.

According to Sara Lawrence-Lightfoot, an educator and sociologist, "Treating someone with respect is not something one can imitate, but something one must embody. Respect as an integral aspect of life, both personal and social, is maintained by the respectful acts of individuals."

Respect starts at home, with parents, or those who are responsible for your wellbeing, and they should get your ultimate respect. Players, as well as coaches, should look to their parents as role models (whenever possible and appropriate, of course.)

Respect isn't just a great idea, it's a biblical one. The fifth of the Ten Commandments is "honor your father and your mother." (Exodus 20:12, NKJV) Any person who assumes a parental or guardianship role in your life, should be given this respect.

Respect begins at home, but should be given to all, especially those who affect your life in some constructive way including elders, relatives, coaches, teammates, administrators, and even referees. These persons will have some effect on your behavior and perspective in one form or another. They will form conceptions about you and the type of person you are based on how well you treat them.

You'll want to have a favorable rapport with those who you interact with consistently, especially those in authoritarian or leadership roles. Some coaches today have abandoned or altogether ignored this important principle.

"Respect is not something one can imitate, but something one must embody."

My seventh year at Cleveland State was another strong year. We were ranked as one of the tops in mid-major. Junior Lomomba was the runner-up player of the year in Wisconsin. He was another top recruit we lost to a high-major program after one year, the Providence Squires.

The next player of this special class was Bryn

Bryn Forbes attacking against the University of Kentucky (Courtesy of Cleveland State University)

Forbes, who transferred to Michigan State in his hometown, after two successful seasons, for personal and family reasons. At present, he plays for the San Antonio Spurs.

The next two players were from south of the Mason Dixon Line, and these acquisitions showed how well we were recruiting outside of our region.

Aaron Scales was a 6'10" post player, who would play and graduate from Cleveland State over the next four years. At the end of his fourth year, he decided to move on as a fifth-year transfer for his final year of competition. He went back to his hometown and attended North Carolina A&T.

Aaron Scales Coaching tips from Coach Waters (Courtesy of Cleveland State University)

The final recruit in this class was Josh Ivory out of Baton Rouge, Louisiana. Josh lasted one year before going the junior college route, a decision we made mutually.

With the addition of these four quality recruits, we became one of the youngest teams in NCAA Division I men's basketball.

The irony? Not one of the four recruits in this class concluded their careers at Cleveland State—all fell victim to the transfer epidemic.

The season started off well, except for a blemish at the University of Michigan, who fashioned a top ten ranking in NCAA Division l. We kept the score somewhat close in the first half due to Anton Grady's robust performance.

As I stated earlier, Anton was a high-major prospect coming out of high school. After he graduated from Cleveland State under the fifth-year transfer rule, he went to the Missouri Valley Conference basketball powerhouse Wichita State. We had now become the poster board for high-major schools needing immediate help to continue competing at a high level.

The schools who recruited the players we had previously drafted into our program had little respect for us and thought nothing of how their recruitment approach affected our team and coaching staff. I think it's safe to say they weren't treating us the way they wanted to be treated.

In terms of our game with the University of Michigan, we were being blitzed in the first ten minutes of the second half until John Beilein, the head coach of Michigan at the time decided to take out his starters and showed some sportsmanship by not trying to run up the score. Coach Beilein displayed respect for our program and treated us the way he would've wanted to be treated.

This was in stark contrast to a high school football coach in Connecticut I read about, who chose to leave his key players in the game for a long time and ran up the score to a 90-0 margin. This was clearly a respect and sportsmanship issue, which prompted a new "score management" policy being enacted by the state. An unnamed source commented on the situation, saying, "It's all a matter of respecting your opponent and the game."

Anton Grady against Stamford University in the NIT (Courtesy of Cleveland State University)

Shortly after the game against Michigan, we finished the pre-season NIT at Robert Morris University. We lost something even more valuable than the game—Anton. He tore a ligament in his knee and he was out for the entire season. He had already undergone surgery twice on the other knee.

This was a major setback for our team. He was our alpha dog, the most dominant person on the team, but it wasn't just Anton's impressive athleticism. It was his strong attitude too.

We were one of the youngest teams in Division I and we'd lost our top player to injury. Our season looked bleak, but we persisted. We held our heads high and centered the rest of the season on character-building and each player's personal growth.

Bryn Forbes and Charlie Lee held everything together for the remainder of the season. They led our team in every category except blocked shots and rebounding, and we were in almost every game we played that season.

Nonetheless, we lost early in the Horizon League Tournament to Loyola of Chicago. We didn't fare well in that contest, but we left the court with our dignity and showed sportsmanship by respecting our opponent, even in defeat.

More importantly, though, we were optimistic about the upcoming season. With a year of experience now behind our young team, Anton's recovery and return, and the host of recruits we were bringing to the next class, we'd be operating at full strength.

The only major player we lost after that season was Junior Lomomba. He took advantage of the transfer rule, and we replaced him with two outstanding transfers of our own who would go on to help us compete for the conference championship over the next two years.

If you're a coach, treating others with respect should be paramount to you and your program, but it should also filter down to your players and anyone connected to your program.

"Respect other people's feelings. It might mean nothing to you, but it could mean everything to them."
—Roy T. Bennett, *Light of the Heart*

PRINCIPLE 5
LOVE UNCONDITIONALLY

*Three things will last forever—faith, hope,
and love—and the greatest of these is love.*
—I Corinthians 13:13

L ife is all about relationships. Whom you choose to associate with and how you choose to behave toward them will have some bearing on who you become. The same is true of your interactions with perfect strangers. Every interaction in some way impacts the type of person you become. All these things together become the sum total of your character and reputation, or what others believe to be true of you.

My wife Bernadette and I have been married forty-eight years. When I said my vows to her all those years ago, I made a commitment to love her unconditionally. That commitment extended to my children and grandchildren when they were born, and if I'm around, it'll cover my great-grandchildren as well.

Marriage is a contract—or, spiritually speaking, a covenant—and it is arguably the most important natural covenant most of us will ever enter. It is a commitment that I renew often in my heart and mind, even if not in my words. I can honestly say, I love her today more than I did when we first fell in love.

Every married person knows that marriage has its challenges and we've had our fair share. Yet our love and respect for each other has gotten us through every trial, especially during the ups and downs of my coaching career.

It has also been my responsibility to demonstrate to my entire family, basketball family included, the love I have for my wife and children. I know how important it is for those who look up to me to see a worthy example of marriage and stability. Back when I was still coaching, I knew the players needed to see marriage modeled in a healthy way so that they will have some barometer by which to measure their own serious relationships.

The players needed to see marriage modeled in a healthy way so that they'll have some barometer by which to measure their own serious relationships.

We started the year preparing ourselves for a foreign tour to Belgium, the Netherlands, and France. Each player in the program was excited and looking forward to the experience. This would be the first-time the NCAA would allow entering freshman and transfer students to participate in a foreign tour before they had completed a year of residency at the university.

For us, this meant every player we added to the program could both travel and play, including transfer students, who had to sit the prior year to meet the residency requirement. Trey Lewis, the lone transfer from Penn State University, would be eligible because he had completed a year of residency before the new rule was put into place.

Trey was an all-state performer and player of the year in Cleveland. He had performed extremely well during his senior year of high school. Since we recruited him early in tenth grade, we'd developed a strong bond, which made it easy for him to decide to transfer to Cleveland State after things didn't work out at Penn State.

We knew from the very beginning that it would be a long shot for Trey to choose Cleveland State over a major college program. But I left the

Trey Lewis scoring against University of Louisville (Courtesy of Cleveland State University)

door open for him to return home if things didn't work out at the high-major university. I also made it quite clear that he could lead our program's ascension to the next level.

One other player came to our program that year by the way of transfer status and his name was Jon Harris. Jon transferred from Miami of Ohio University with only one year of eligibility due to a family medical crisis. His family lived in the area, so he would be coming back home.

Jon was a three-year starter at Miami of Ohio and one of their top scorers, making his transfer somewhat of a surprise. But his coach—the late Charlie Coles—was on board, since Jon was leaving for credible reasons. But Jon had to petition the NCAA for a family medical hardship waiver to be able to play immediately. They granted his request and he was reinstated at the start of the summer semester.

The final player came to us from Polk Junior College, Ismaila Dauda, known as I.D. The seven-foot post player also joined us on the trip, and was exactly what we needed. In addition, each participating student-athlete could have an extra ten days of practice during the summer to prepare themselves for the competition.

There was much more to be gained from this international trip than simply playing basketball. I wanted our players to have an immersive learning and cultural experience that they would remember for the rest of their lives.

For most people, traveling abroad is an unforgettable venture into awe-inspiring situations and surroundings, if for no other reason than you are in completely unfamiliar territory. But certain factors make these trips even more remarkable.

Obviously, the players are the reason for the trip, but the coaches, parents, and others invited to support or assist also make the trip a memorable experience.

In terms of unconditional family love, I can think of no better example to share than Joe and Nina Lewis, Trey's parents, who joined us on the trip.

Joe and Nina were loving, playful, and respectful toward one another. The way they connected and related to one another gave our players and coaches an intimate look at how a husband should honor and esteem his wife in public. They genuinely enjoyed being in each other's company. Joe and Nina's presence reinforced indispensable life lessons regarding family values, marital devotion, and unconditional love.

Throughout the trip, each player treated my wife with the utmost respect, treating her as the maternal figure of the team. While I couldn't say it unequivocally, I would like to believe they treated her this way, at least in part, because they

Bernadette Waters with Coach and Team

Lisa Hehman Academic Coordinator at CSU (Courtesy of Cleveland State University)

saw how I treated her, with affection, adoration, and admiration.

Another key person in our program who joined us on our trip was our academic coordinator, Lisa Hehman. Lisa had been with us for several years and her relationship with the players was crucial.

Lisa's significant-other Kevin joined us on the trip as well. One evening, our entire party went out to eat together. We enjoyed our meals, swapped stories, and were getting ready to wrap up for the night when Kevin took me aside and said he would ask Lisa for her hand in marriage during our trip.

The next day, when we were visiting the Eiffel Tower, in true chivalrous form, with the landmark wrought iron

structure doubling as décor for the Parisian skyline and the stage for his proposal, Kevin got down on one knee and asked Lisa to be his wife.

Unequivocally, this was Kevin and Lisa's special moment, but we were a part of it, if only as

Coach and Mrs. Waters at Eiffel Tower

onlookers, and we were grateful to be witnesses. We'd been privy to an authentic expression of their unconditional love and commitment to each other.

Overall, the trip went well. Our players learned about and experienced the cultures of other countries. On top of that, we competed very well, as we won all four games during the competition portion of the trip, and discovered the importance of international spirit in competition.

One of my primary goals for this trip was for our players to come together, old and new, and form a more cohesive group. I wanted them to grow close enough to care about looking out for and taking care of each other. By the time we left, I truly felt we fulfilled this goal, while also growing in character and experiencing unconditional love with one another.

Once we returned to the States, we needed to build the bond we'd formed while overseas. We continued to spend quality time together, which began with a Thanksgiving meal at the Lewis' home. Our basketball team joined Trey's entire family for dinner, and once again, the Lewis' showed our players the meaning of genuine family love. I was keenly aware some of our players had never seen what this looked like, or more significantly, experienced what it felt like to be surrounded by so much love.

We stayed united throughout the non-conference season. In fact, a week before this meal, we played a nationally televised game against the University of Kentucky, a top-ten ranked team in NCAA Division I.

The game went down to the final moments. We had led the entire contest, that is, until the last two minutes, which proved to be decisive. We made some critical errors that unfortunately, cost us the game.

Nonetheless, we left Lexington, Kentucky assured that we had given our best effort, heartened by Kentucky fans as they acknowledged our performance with a standing ovation.

We parlayed our play that evening into a successful non-conference season, as well as conference play. Our goal was to win the conference championship and we were right on target. For the next two years, we would play for the regular season conference championship at our place, with the winner having the opportunity to host the conference tournament.

Coach Waters shakes hands with Coach Calipari at Kentucky (Courtesy of Cleveland State University)

In both instances, we came up short.

But then, our chances became even slimmer when Bryn Forbes succumbed to a stomach virus the morning of the game. He was our leading scorer and the best three-point shooter in our conference, so we knew that a formidable task lay ahead when we heard he was scratched from the lineup. This would be the equivalent to losing Steph Curry of the Golden State Warriors in the NBA Finals.

I remember all the things we did leading up to that game to get our minds right. We scheduled our Success Class on the Thursday before our Saturday game to remain focused.

Success Class was a course I created to help our players define success for themselves, and give them constructive perspectives to frame difficult conditions or situations. That day, to keep us grounded, Success Class was designed to divert our attention away from the game.

In Success Class, I would assign a book for the players to reference throughout the year to give them insight on how to handle the various circumstances they would face in their lives. That year, I chose Tony Dungy's book, *Quiet Strength*.

I won't offer any spoilers in case you haven't read it but hope to. This book really helped us think differently about our lives when we considered the things Coach Dungy had to go through with his family.

On the other hand, what helped Coach Dungy and his family get through each ordeal was their unconditional love for one another. Bryn's absence in such a crucial contest gave us an opportunity to apply what we had learned from *Quiet Strength*, to show love and be there to lean on each other.

We lost the contest that night and the semi-final game in the Horizon League Tournament, but going through each trial helped our team get better in areas which are still beneficial today.

As coaches, we have a responsibility to show and provide unconditional love to everyone we consider part of our families. For many, our example may be the only one they'll be able to relate to during their real-life experiences. The love we show to our spouses and families is exactly what our players and fellow coaches need and are looking for today.

PRINCIPLE 6
WORK HARD AT WHAT MATTERS

There is no substitute for hard work.
—**Thomas Edison**, American Inventor

Once again, we were considered frontrunners in the Horizon League, even though we had lost four important parts of our machine.

Bryn Forbes had transferred to Michigan State in his hometown of Lansing, due to a family hardship. Sebastian Douglas decided not to play his fifth year because of a complication to his surgically repaired knee. I.D. transferred to North Florida University to be closer to his guardian, while Jon Harris graduated in the spring of that year and later took his talents overseas to play professionally.

One would think that, losing two of our leading scorers in Bryn and Jon, our most dominant defender and team leader in Sebastian, and an inside presence in I.D., our chances of competing for a title would be slim to none.

But we had two things going in our favor. The first thing was the talent we had returning, including a skilled transfer student from Creighton University, a Big East Conference school. His name was Andre Yates, and he was coming off a red-shirt year. He had attended the same high school that Norris Cole and Aaron Poque attended. Andre was player of the year in Dayton and a Division IV state champion his senior year.

The second thing was our work ethic. Our focus on and commitment to working hard was a distinguishing quality of our program that we had become known for throughout the league. Thus, even with our losses, opponents were still intimidated by our presence. Other coaches classified us with the elite.

The effort you put forth will determine the outcome of what you pursue. I learned this lesson from my father, who worked hard at everything he ever accomplished.

He was an interior and exterior decorator by trade, a profession he acquired in the early 1900s. In those days, there was a direct correlation between how hard you worked and the amount of food there would be on the table, or whether there would be food at all.

Those were The Great Depression years, so work was not easy to find. But my father was college-educated, and had picked up the trade through his formal instruction. It was one of the few trades a black man could learn in those days.

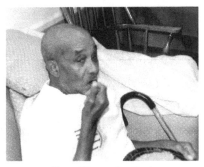

Albert Waters Sr. Father of Coach Waters

Decorating was a manual trade back then; people were hired for their skill, as well as their work ethic. Forty years in, he was a master of his craft, but not only that, his work ethic was a constant. He was reliable, and because I had no choice but to witness this every day growing up, it became a part of my makeup. I didn't know any other way. Working hard at what mattered was the norm, and being able to feed your family, as a man, mattered more than anything.

———

God doesn't give everyone equal gifts and talents, but He does give everyone the ability to work hard...

———

Unsurprisingly then, this philosophy became the one I employed and endorsed throughout my entire coaching career, and my teams became known for it. When we faced an opponent, regardless of the outcome, they would come away saying, "Boy, do they play hard."

What they were really acknowledging was how hard we worked. God doesn't give everyone equal gifts and talents, but He does give everyone the ability to work hard, and it's up to us to choose where we want to put the work in.

For example, when two teams on the court are equal in talent, the team that plays the hardest will usually have an advantage in a close contest. The same principle applies to recruiting a student-athlete. The coach who puts in the most time and work, the one who pays attention, who does their homework, who travels a little further and stays a little longer, will *usually* be the one with better results, notwithstanding unethical strategies or competing coaches being at a much higher level.

This is the reason ethics and values should be the heart of a character coach's recruiting methodology. Today, certain coaches are being singled out for recruiting unethically or down right cheating to gain an advantage. We'll discuss this more in later chapters, but I believe there is no place in our profession nor in other college sports for this to be accepted or tolerated. When a coach recruits through corrupt means, not only does he cheat the profession, but himself and the players he's recruiting along with it.

This year, we brought in a diverse and large recruiting class, four quality freshman and two transfers. Vinny Zollo was a four-two-four transfer; he started out at a four-year institution, transferred to a two-year institution, and finished at Cleveland State, a four-year institution.

Kaza Keane from Toronto, Canada transferred from Illinois State University on an NCAA-approved family medical hardship waiver. He was able to play immediately with two years of eligibility remaining.

The freshman group consisted of Kenny Carpenter and Terrell Hales, who were Detroit PSL products, and Jonathan Jansen from Australia via a Philadelphia Prep School. We also added Tim Hasenberger as a walk-on from Munich, Germany to complete the four-person freshman class. Tim played for a Cleveland-based AAU program operated by Dennis Barba, a friend to the program.

These six recruits, as well as Andre Yates, all contributed meaningfully to the program that year. Character development was already important to each of them, and their value-based moral fiber strengthened our system.

Our major contributors were the five players who had significant playing time the previous year. They showed the way to the newcomers and were exemplars of our integrity-focused, hardworking culture, a culture that characterized Cleveland State Basketball.

Three games somewhat defined the outcome of our season. A tough loss at Detroit Mercy on a thirty-foot shot by Juan Howard Jr., whose father had been a standout at the University of Michigan and an NBA all-star. We led the game the entire way, but that final desperation shot sealed our fate.

The next game that defined our season was a nationally televised road win against the University of Wisconsin-Green Bay, a tri-leader for the regular-season title. This was a place where we'd had difficulty winning in the past, but in this game, we knocked them out of contention to make it a two-team race.

The last game was a showdown amongst Valparaiso University, Valpo for short. It ended with us suffering a closing minute defeat, which gave them the regular season championship and the home-court advantage during the Horizon League Tournament.

We worked hard the entire game. We gave it everything we had, but sometimes, the team that works the hardest just may not have enough that game, especially when two teams are evenly matched.

We did, however, redeem ourselves during the quarter-final matchup against Detroit Mercy, where we single-handedly dominated them on Valpo's court.

Then, we faced Valpo in the semi-finals, where they prevailed in the last ten seconds. We had our opportunities, but missed free throws with three seconds left on the clock, ending our chances. Once again, we played extremely hard but came up short.

We were later invited to the CBI Tournament, similar to the tournament we went to the year prior and defeated

Western Michigan University on the road in the first round, where Charlie Lee played his best game as a Viking, scoring thirty-five points. But we lost the contest in the second round at New Jersey Institute without two of our major contributors, Charlie Lee for personal reasons and Trey Lewis due to an injury.

For the most part, the season went as expected, apart from the number of close games we lost in the final moments, costing us a conference championship and an NCAA appearance. These were always the hardest losses to reconcile. Nonetheless, our work ethic never wavered, from the players to the coaching staff, which left an impression on that season.

Charlie Lee competes during Cleveland State Game (Courtesy of Cleveland State University)

My father would have been proud, God rest his soul. I only hope that every member of our program, players and coaches alike, realize the importance of working hard at what matters throughout their lives, which I believe is a great equalizer in life.

PRINCIPLE 7
VALUE LOYALTY

*"Loyalty isn't grey. It's black and white. You're
either loyal completely, or not loyal at all."*

—Anonymous

The spring before my tenth season at Cleveland State was tough and difficult to overcome.

We had lost two of the top players in the conference, along with an important starter, who was a seasoned veteran. All three had a season of competition remaining and were predicted to have an outstanding year. These losses, coupled with the losses of two other four-year players, Charlie Lee and Marlin Mason, who were graduating, depleted us of an entire starting lineup. We'd have to start from scratch with limited to no experience on our roster.

Trey Lewis and Anton Grady would have been first team all-conference players returning from the past year with a great amount of experience. But both players elected to take their talents elsewhere for their fifth and final year of eligibility.

This brings to mind the concept of loyalty and what it means to different people. One definition is the commitment one makes to a cause, group, or specific persons, which connotes feelings of devotion or obligation to someone or something, revealing the value of loyalty.

Other definitions describe loyalty as faithfulness to something or someone to which one is bound by pledge or duty, and the faithfulness to a commitment or obligation with unwavering allegiance. All these definitions get at the gist of loyalty—a commitment to someone or something.

Norris Cole and President Berkman show loyalty to Cleveland State (Courtesy of Cleveland State University)

Cassandra Clare, in her young adult novel *Clockwork Princess*, says this:

> "Is loyalty still a commendable quality when it is misdirected?
>
> ...
>
> I think when we make choices—for each choice is individual of the choices we have made before—we must examine not only our reasons for making them, but what result they will have and whether good people will be hurt by our decisions."

What wise words!

Loyalty to the wrong cause, or lack of loyalty altogether, can have detrimental consequences for an individual and those connected to him or her.

We live in a time when loyalty has less value. In all walks of life people are treating loyalty like a commodity to be traded rather than a value to be upheld.

In college basketball, this unfortunate trend has not gone unnoticed. Administrations are less committed to the coaches they've hired to lead their programs. Today, administrators, and colleges show loyalty to only those coaches who are having success on the court winning ball games. Success in the classroom and players' personal growth and development play second fiddle, if they come into play at all. Far more important are coaches having success in their sport and keeping supporters happy.

(Dis)loyalty is also an issue for college coaches. Some are less committed to their institutions and even their own players. For the right price or the lure of acclaim they may receive from success elsewhere, they will abandon their previous commitments. They change schools like a mother changing the diaper of her newborn baby.

But the biggest victims of the loyalty problem, by far, are the players, who are following the examples of all the disloyal adults they regard as role models. Players are transferring from school to school starting at an early age, and carrying that attitude into college, where we have over a thousand transfers each year.

Summer league AAU teams are dealing with this epidemic on a recurrent basis. Loyalty does not exist in the summer programs today for many reasons. One of those reasons - the players are not being allowed to perform the way they want. Another reason—the players did not receive the perks they have been promised. And still another - the parents getting involved in the decision-making and making choices that they feel best benefit them, not necessarily their child.

This behavior has been tolerated at the AAU level for such a long time that it affects high school coaches' ability to coach and lead their players. I feel so sorry for the kids today, who are being catered to in ways that far surpass the ways in which kids were accommodated in the past, which makes loyalty, in their view, a thing of the past.

———

I feel so sorry for the kids today, who are being catered to in ways that far surpass the ways in which kids were accommodated in the past, which makes loyalty, in their view, a thing of the past.

———

Connect the dots to everyone involved in the process and you'll see that something is broken and in desperate need of repair. The NCAA is attempting to address and correct this issue, with the introduction of legislation that is being deliberated by their newly formed commission. However, until something official is sanctioned, it will be left to us as coaches, administrators, parents, and players to elevate loyalty to the standard it once was. We need to embrace it as a part of who we are as people of character, who care about the integrity of the profession.

Since most of this team was in its first and second year of eligibility, loyalty was in its nascence. It was our responsibility to help our revamped team understand the meaning of this principle.

We brought in five new players and a red-shirt transfer who sat out the previous year. Bobby Word was the transfer from Oral Roberts, who was considered one of the better shooters in their conference.

The five new faces were all freshmen. Robert Edwards was the marque recruit in that class. He was an all-state performer out of Cass Tech in Detroit, the school that produced Marlin Mason and Kenny Carpenter.

Jibri Blount was out of Pittsburg, Pennsylvania, but he had played at St. Vincent-St. Mary's in Akron, Ohio, the same school that produced LeBron James. Jibri was also the son of the Hall of Famer Mel Blount of the Pittsburg Steelers. What genes!

The next newbie was Jeron Rogers out of Farmington, Michigan, who also had some good genes. Jeron's father, Carlos Rogers, was an NBA first-round draft pick.

The two other freshmen were walk-ons and they contributed a great deal to the team that season. Daniel Levitt from Montreal, Quebec, who spent one year of prep school in the states at New Hampton Prep in New Hampshire, and Nelson Maxwell a Cleveland product out of Orange High School.

This young team had a tough time in the early goings. We went on a trip to Cancun, Mexico to start the beginning of the non-conference season. On the bright side, we had an extraordinary time and we came away with a victory over Rider University of the MAAC to finish the trip. The rest of the non-conference games were up and down. We even had to change the line up several times to find a rhythm that worked.

Overall, it was a solid learning experience for our young team, which we were grateful for. Now, we faced what I considered to be a perfect storm.

We all face storms in our lives, but a *perfect* storm—well, that's different than the run-of-the-mill storms which maturity prepares you to expect in life. In a perfect storm, not only does it feel as though nothing is flowing in your favor, it feels like everything is going *against* you.

We already had an inexperienced group but add to that a portion of our home games being played at an unfamiliar location, the Quicken Loans Arena, the Cleveland Cavaliers' homecourt, and the storm was just overwhelming. Our first year at that facility turned out to be an arduous challenge, and truly not worth the headaches. We lost our home-court advantage and with it, a great deal of this young team's confidence.

Another leg of the storm was all the new college game rule changes, which affected our style of play. It took the entire season for our team to adjust to the officiating and try to surmount our disadvantages.

Our league was mostly filled with juniors and seniors, which made it a very experienced conference for us to compete in, and this put us a step behind the other teams.

But we were tenacious. We competed in every contest and we won some games that we were not expected to win. The storm was tapering off and one thing brought closure to our season: the post-season Horizon League Tournament being held at a neutral site instead of at the regular season league winner's site.

This change was devised to create more tournament excitement and to add more student and community involvement. The change in venue removed homecourt advantage, giving each team an equal chance of winning the tournament.

And as if to prove this change was as effective as it was created to be, the third-place team, a team in Wisconsin, Green Bay that had never won the Horizon League Tournament, earned the rights. They ended up winning the championship that year and went on to the NCAA Tournament, something that was highly unlikely to have happened had they been playing against a team with homecourt advantage.

But the most important thing for me was the players' and coaches' commitment to the program and the process under the pressures they were facing. I viewed their commitment as a form of loyalty. This is the brand of loyalty that coaches need to show in the profession and to each other.

Mario Cuomo, a Former Governor of New York said this about David Robinson, an NBA great, "David Robinson chose to stay at Navy. He talked about commitment, loyalty, and values. I wonder how many of us would choose these virtues rather than the chance of becoming a millionaire, especially if you were a college sophomore when you had to make the choice?"

Are you a person who values and demonstrates loyalty? If not, you have become a part of the problem and not a part of the solution. I challenge you to reconsider your position, to think of those whom you lead and love, and ask yourself if the price of disloyalty is worth what it'll cost you in character.

PRINCIPLE 8
EMPOWER AND SERVE

Leaders become great not because of their power,
but because of their ability to empower others.
—**John Maxwell**, American Author, Speaker, and Pastor

My final year of coaching at Cleveland State came as a bit of a surprise. The previous year, I had mentioned to my athletic director John Parry, if things didn't take place the way I expected them that year, then I would consider retiring and forgo my final year of the contract.

John was the former athletic director of Butler University during the beginning of their glory years, before taking over for Lee Reed at Cleveland State. Therefore, he was knowledgeable about situations like the one I was in.

John was on board with the decision and was committed to doing what was necessary, should it become necessary. He wanted me to end my career on a positive note and on my own terms. The only major concern I had was my coaching staff and their wellbeing, should I decide to opt out my final year. I had always been committed to serving and empowering the people who worked under me, so I wanted to ensure that each coach on my staff would land on their feet in an ideal spot. From that moment on, I was dedicated to serving them in a way I hadn't had to before. I needed to make sure I set them up for success, only this time, without me.

The academic year was about to begin, and all the players were set and in the program. We had made a significant decision in the spring regarding our recruiting direction. We elected to go the junior college route to increase our scoring and to add more experience to a team that was still somewhat young, comparatively. We needed to have an immediate impact if we wanted to compete in a league that was looking for a frontrunner.

I also wanted to create a solution for the fifth-year transfer dilemma that was plaguing the mid-major schools. We agreed that if we could recruit players who had limited choices once they entered our institution for their final two years, we would have the upper hand. This would decrease the likelihood of losing our fifth-year players to high-major programs that were pilfering our mid-major talent.

We brought in three junior-college players with good skills and the ability to score, but I had one stipulation in their recruitment, and by now, you probably already know what it was. They all had to exemplify character and integrity. Because of my adverse experience with junior college players, we struggled with having more than two at a time. Let me explain, lest I paint all junior college players with a broad, biased brush.

In my experience, many players opt for junior college over a four-year institution because there is an obstacle, be it academic underperformance, underdeveloped skills, or personal issues. Sure, these obstacles can be surmounted, but at what rate? For certain programs, the risk is not worth the reward.

Some of the junior college players I had in the past struggled with character issues. The kind of freedom afforded by a junior college environment can be too much for some to handle. By nature of its structure, there is less accountability than traditional four-year college environments, and young men, especially young men who are immature, need accountability.

But ultimately, I incorporated this stipulation because I felt it would give us a better chance of getting it right. Anthony Wright was from Harcum College in Pennsylvania and led his team to the National Junior College Tournament in Hutchinson, Kansas. He was multi-talented, as he was one of the top scorers and led his team in assists and steals from the forward position.

Gavin Pepper out of Laramie Junior College was one of the top scoring guards in junior college. He was a talented point guard and led his team to the regional finals before bowing out to the top team in the tournament. Gavin did not have the opportunity to play this season, due to a foot injury that sidelined him for the entire year.

That summer, after I announced my retirement, he transferred to Central Michigan University. I only wish I would have had the opportunity to coach him that season.

The last junior college player was JaMarcus Hairston from Louisburg Junior College in North Carolina, known as J-Mac. J-Mac led his team to the Junior College National Tournament in Division II and was one of the top three-point shooters, especially for a post player.

Anthony and J-Mac graduated from Cleveland State and represented themselves well. I was extremely proud of my staff. I had challenged and empowered them to recruit the right junior college players, and they'd spent long hours working, finding young men with the right character traits, who would fit into our young culture.

Now it was my responsibility to provide the support
and service they needed to make this situation work
under any circumstances. I also needed to empower my

coaches so that they felt in control of the situation,
not like the previous time four years earlier.

During the year, I would put them in situations where they would direct the outcome of planned programs, such as our mentor and player development programs. The coaches who oversaw these programs felt emboldened to take control of every stage of the project. Every step they took was a step closer to heading their own program when it was time.

The three junior college recruits were not alone in this recruiting class. We also added three other high school prospects. Evan Clayborn out of Dayton, Ohio was a physical post player from Thurgood Marshall. Kash Thomas out of Montreal, Quebec, was an all-provincial player and led his team to the Provincial Championship in Montreal. The last player in the class was Andy Lucien, a preferred walk-on from North Olmstead High School in the Cleveland area. Andy had boundless potential and was scheduled to receive a scholarship the following year. He decided to transfer to a Division II school in the area after I announced my retirement that spring.

This season started out with some early impressive wins in the non-conference. We also performed much better in the early games played at the Quicken Loans Arena. We decreased the number of games we played there, bearing in mind the issues we experienced the previous year.

This season followed the path of the prior season when you compare wins and losses, but we were much more competitive, which gave us the opportunity to win almost every contest. The conference games were challenging to be sure, but the scores were often close, making them exciting to watch and to experience.

Once the Horizon League tournament started in Detroit, this would be the last time we could play our post season tournament in the Joe Louis Arena. They were leveling the facility and moving to a new site, downtown at the Little Caesar Arena, which is perpendicular to the Ford Fieldhouse and the Co-America Park Stadium, forming a massive sports complex. Consequently, our presence at this site was short lived, but the persona was still there. This would also be the last season for the Detroit Red Wings of the NHL at this site, their original location as well, so a great deal of history would be leaving this building.

We lost to our crosstown rival Youngstown State in the closing minutes of the first round of the tournament, which concluded my tenure as a head coach at Cleveland State. It was the last game I coached.

Two weeks later, I announced my retirement from Cleveland State, and with that announcement, forty-three years of coaching came to an end.

So, what about the rest of my staff that I had poured into for many years? Much to my delight, they all landed jobs. My efforts toward empowerment and servanthood culminated with my staff being taken care of.

Larry DeSimpelare, my longtime assistant for over twenty years, became the commissioner of the Crossroads League of the National Association of Intercollegiate Athletics (NAIA), a position he was well prepared for. When I learned of his appointment, I reflected on my service to him, and hoped that it helped him understand the importance of serving others.

Cornelius Jackson, Corn as we called him, transitioned to the top assistant position at Marshall University, his alma mater. Corn was destined to move forward in this profession because he truly modeled a character coach. I did my best to help him cultivate that quality, and hoped he considered himself a better man for it.

2016-17 Cleveland State Basketball Staff (Courtesy of Cleveland State University)

Jermaine Henderson, the longtime assistant to the late Charlie Coles, had a choice between becoming an athletic director in Columbus, Ohio, his hometown, or being an assistant coach at Kansas State. Would you believe he chose the latter?

I know he had his handprint all over the run Kansas State made in the NCAA Tournament this season. Even today, we still talk about how highly we regarded service and empowerment to the success and professional development of our staff during his brief time at Cleveland State.

The spring period after my announcement was marvelous. The university held a retirement reception on my behalf. I could understand the athletic department doing this, but the entire university? That was unheard of. It was…marvelous!

The commencement ceremony was even more magnificent. The president of the university, Ronald Berkman, presented me with the President's Medal, Cleveland State's most prestigious non-academic recognition, marking the first time a non-faculty member had been awarded this esteemed honor.

President Berkman Medal Presentation at Graduation (Courtesy of Cleveland State University)

I retired as the all-time winningest coach in program history, as well as having an academic performance rate in the top ten percent nationally among NCAA universities.

The president's service to me during our time together is something I will remember for the remainder of my life.

The final commitment that I spent my time on that year was servicing the international coaches in Europe. I traveled to Greece in July to conduct a clinic for coaches there to strengthen their coaching skills and knowledge of the game with substantive, tested, and proven, teaching and training. It was a wonderful experience.

I worked with over one hundred coaches and players during a two-day clinic designed to improve their coaching skills. Although the program was for them, it increased my awareness in foreign diplomacy. It was ultimately my way of serving other coaches, by adding to their knowledge and understanding of the profession that I cherish.

All coaches should be committed to serving and empowering any coach under their supervision. This is an integral part of the process when developing other character coaches.

PRINCIPLE 9
HONOR THE PROFESSION

I would prefer even to fail with
honor than win by cheating.
—**Sophocles**, Ancient Greek Dramatist
and Tragedian (496–406 B.C.)

One morning in November of 2017, I was watching ESPN and listened as a commentator narrated a story about the corrupt recruiting practices of several college basketball coaches, who had now come to heel because of their exposure.

This has gotten out of hand, I thought, echoing the reporting journalist's sentiments, and at that moment, I felt compelled to get involved in some way.

The college basketball profession was taking a hit now that salacious details of the corruption were making their way to the airwaves. These scandals raised the eyebrows of many university presidents, athletic directors, coaches, as well as student-athletes. Outsiders would have to decipher truth from myth, as facts got mixed in with broad speculation about what exactly had been taking place.

Many connected parties had willfully participated in the shady dealings, from shoe companies, sports agencies, and AAU programs, to college coaches, players, and parents. There was blame to be shared on both sides of the equation and while their seemed to be involvement at every level to some extent, the FBI, who was leading the investigation, didn't directly accuse anyone.

But why was the FBI involved in college athletic matters anyway? My thought is that the FBI believed federal offenses may have been committed by certain parties, falling under their jurisdiction. The circumstances required special attention. Eventually, the FBI released a comprehensive report to the media, detailing the conclusion of their lengthy investigation.

This investigation, coupled with the trainer scandals at certain schools and the Olympic competition issues, which also cited some basketball players, cast college athletics into a downward spiral—at least, that was the perception.

To be clear, most of the incidences were isolated cases. But a dark cloud covered collegiate athletics as a whole, nonetheless. In the case of basketball, media reports had convinced people that many players and programs in Division I had been implicated in this investigation. This was not the case, however; very few were involved. Still, the narrative tarnished the entire sport.

Even though, most of the incidences were isolated cases,
a dark cloud was starting to cover college athletics.

I was taught early in my career to never commit illegal or unethical behavior inside or outside the profession. The character coaches who provided an example for me rejected unethical practices, and so did I. Cheating erode trust, and you can't have a solid system or program without trust, thus, cheating should not be tolerated.

Although I had officially retired on June 30th, you could say that I was distracted from fully embracing it by all the issues that were being discussed nationally in college basketball. Plus, I was still a board member of the National Association of Basketball Coaches (NABC).

The NABC has been in existence for over ninety years and is headed by Executive Director Jim Haney. It's the backbone of college basketball, but operates under the authority of the NCAA. This organization, under Jim Haney's leadership, has done significant work to further various causes and advance the missions of college basketball coaches. College basketball would not be as prevalent as it is today if it wasn't for the vision of Jim Haney and the support of the NABC.

Condoleezza Rice Chairperson of the NCAA College Basketball Commission (Courtesy of U.S. Department of State)

Because I had retired, I had time to focus on these improprieties. The NABC was indirectly involved with the coaches, the FBI investigation, and the newly assembled commission of the NCAA, headed by former U. S. Secretary of State Condoleezza Rice.

The commission's purpose was to evaluate men's college basketball and determine if the current legislation fit the landscape. Then, after listening to designated brokers in the profession, the commission's responsibility was to provide recommendations for improvement.

This group of stakeholders included each party I mentioned earlier in the chapter, but not the NABC. They were allowed and encouraged, however, to provide recommendations to the commission. So, the NABC formed an ad hoc committee that would listen to all the suggestions of each board member, then draft recommendations to present to the commission.

After much collaboration and a thorough review, the commission submitted the ideas they thought would help improve the profession, and to help the powers-that-be gain more control over men's college basketball. Several of the recommendations presented by the NABC committee were used in the final recommendations, which Dr. Rice read on national television to Mark Emmert, the president of the NCAA, and the NCAA governing body.

When I heard these recommendations, I effectively put my retirement on hold. My discussions with Jim Haney included conversations about what I could do professionally to help college coaches in the sport.

I began by connecting with Curtis Hollomon, the director of NCAA Leadership Development. I wanted to get directly involved with their Men's Basketball Coaches Academy. He was eager to have me as part of his program in Tampa, the city I now call home.

This would be the first time the Coaches Academy provided an in-service seminar for college basketball coaches. There have been similar activities provided by other programs, such as the ACE Program (Achieving Coaching Excellence), housed by both the NCAA and the Black Coaches Association for several years, as well as the Vella Seven Program, once sponsored by Nike, but nothing as informative and inclusive as this seminar.

I have always felt that development for college coaches is critical to help enhance the skills and knowledge of those in the profession. I've long witnessed the inexpedient way that coaches enter the profession with such limited experience. The time I spent presenting and working with coaches at the academy was invaluable—worth every minute, even in my retirement.

Although it appeared that college basketball was going through a watershed moment, with the state of the game at its highest level of notoriety, at its core, it was still intact.

The NCAA Final Four Men's Championship was a financial success, and it was entertaining as well. Four quality teams made it to the Final Four: Loyola, Villanova, Michigan, and Kansas. The latter three are elite universities in college sports and some think of them as "Blue Bloods" in the game of basketball. By contrast, Loyola of Chicago was considered to be the Cinderella team of the tournament. Overall, the country could not have had a better event.

Villanova defeated Kansas in the semi-finals, while Michigan beat Loyola in an exciting game. When I looked out on the court, I saw four teams with similar attributes and styles. Each had quality veterans, each were outstanding passing teams, and each were committed to shooting the long ball, the three-point shot.

What was even more obvious was their ability to excel on both sides of the court. This was no doubt an effect of the rule changes and the commitment to allow the game to be played in a free-flowing manner.

The atmosphere was exhilarating and San Antonio, Texas was the ideal site to host a tournament of this magnitude. My wife and I enjoyed our time in San Antonio, and in my opinion, it had been the best location on the Final Four circuit. The weather was great, the lodging was excellent, the restaurant eating was superb, and the Riverwalk was a joy.

Villanova overwhelmed Michigan during the second half of the championship game, and at times, it looked as though Jay Wright, the head coach of Villanova, and his talented bunch, were putting on a clinic. Donte DiVincenzo, an up-and-coming underclassman had an outstanding performance and was voted the game's MVP.

Each team in the Final Four was committed to doing things the right way, with no thought of cheating the game nor the players in any way.

So…what now? Where does men's college basketball go from here?

The commission seems to have some well-considered answers, but it will take time, since they are still finalizing recommendations. We must be patient, and in the interim, work together in support of the powers-that-be.

But since the indictments, there have been federal subpoenas and continued investigations, firing within college basketball programs, and more recently, convictions of wire fraud and conspiracy to commit wire fraud handed down to an executive of the world's second-largest sportswear manufacturer, a consultant to the same, and an aspiring sports agent.[3]

As coaches, one thing we should never do is cheat our profession, nor the future of the *kids whose lives we have in our hands.*

While we have our work cut out for us just to get back on track, the wheels are in motion, and the rails are straight lines pointing to where we want this profession to be.

It is now up to all of us, the coaches, university administrations, the NBA, AAU organizations, the sports agencies, the shoe companies, the parents, and the student-athletes to uphold a moral standard and do things the right way.

---

3   https://www.courier-journal.com/story/sports/college/
louisville/2018/10/24/fbi-hoops-trial-guilty-verdict-louisville-
basketball-ncaa/1724487002/

PRINCIPLE 10
LEAVE A CHARACTER LEGACY

The greatest legacy one can pass on to one's children and grandchildren is not money or other material things accumulated in one's life, but rather a legacy of character and faith.

—**Billy Graham**, American Christian Evangelist

What do you think it means to leave a legacy?

Author and motivational speaker Jim Rohn say, "All good men and women must take responsibility to create legacies that will take the next generation to a level we could only imagine."

I agree with Jim Rohn that this is true, especially when it comes to college sports.

Israelmore Ayivor, an inspirational writer and life skill entrepreneur, renders it this way, "You were created and designed in a special form to leave in the world something that did not exist before you were born!"

Jim Wink Ferris State University (Courtesy of Ferris State University)

Leaving a character legacy is bigger than leaving a traditional legacy. The first college coach who trained me left me with a character legacy, and even though I was trained by numerous character coaches throughout my career, I will never forget Jim Wink.

Jim was my college coach at Ferris State University in the 1970s, and a true character coach. He gave me my first coaching job at Ferris State. He taught me the true meaning of being a character-driven coach. Jim not only talked about character, he walked and lived it every day of his life.

When he passed away, he left a legacy for me and many others to honor through our choices and actions. His headstone should read, "A man of true character."

After retiring, I had been out of coaching for most of the year, but I was still following the games, especially Cleveland State's. My own legacy was visible among the players who returned that season.

Our program of the past was built around three important disciplines— character, hard work, and defense. Later in our program, we rephrased hard work as mental and physical toughness, since toughness incorporated hard work. At the end of that season, these three disciplines were tested and produced amazing results, results far greater than most would imagine.

Cleveland State was scheduled to go up against Youngstown State for a play-in game to determine who would be the eighth seed in an eight-team Horizon League tournament. CSU defeated Youngstown State on a missed lay-up in the closing seconds. Youngstown could probably feel the pressure of Cleveland State's defense, the past staple of Cleveland State basketball, closing in on them. We coined a phrase based on this approach, "Offense wins games, but defense wins championships."

The two teams had split two games during the regular season in the closing seconds, so this was not an uncommon situation. The next game was against Northern Kentucky, the number-one seed in the tournament and the tournament winner from the year before. They had defeated Cleveland State by double digits during two early regular season contests.

Adding fuel to the fire, Northern Kentucky was the number one offensive team in the conference. But Cleveland State's defense prevailed once again, holding Northern

Kentucky to forty-two percent and five of twenty-four from the three-point arc, which allowed Cleveland State to close them out in the final moments, the essence of their defensive legacy.

In the semi-final game, Cleveland State went up against Oakland University, another one of the top teams in the conference. They played at Little Caesars Arena in Detroit, basically giving Oakland homecourt advantage because of how close we were to their hometown. Oakland had also defeated Cleveland State by double digits both times in the regular season. However, this time was different. Cleveland State had a new focus, and that focus was defense.

The legacy continued as Cleveland State put on a defensive performance unmatched by any other team in the tournament. They outlasted Oakland and shut down their inside presence against one of the best post players in the conference, Jalen Hayes. They held him scoreless most of the second half after he led his team in scoring during the first half. They also shut down the leading scorer in the conference, Kendrick Nunn, who was seven of twenty-four for the game.

Cleveland State was on track to do something that no one thought they could do, except them—overcome all odds and win the Horizon League Championship.

I believe this was all made possible due to their commitment and new focus on a strength they possessed all along, their defensive prowess. This was a discipline my coaching staff and I had instilled in our players the minute they reached our campus, so my departure didn't and couldn't stop this progression; it was just a matter of when it would surface.

Cleveland State was about to play in the championship game with nothing to lose. I was immensely proud of them and laser-focused on the outcome, but unfortunately, they ran out of gas and were defeated by Wright State. They just didn't have enough in the tank to finish the dream. But they were dignified in their defeat. They showed character and proved once again that offense can help you win games, but defense will get you to the championship with the opportunity to win it all.

This group of seniors and a few underclassmen made their mark in the Horizon League Tournament, which allowed most of them to end the season and finish their college careers on a high note. I have always believed when a team enters a tournament healthy, hot, and hungry, which I called the Three H's of tournament success, they have a better chance of going all the way.

I knew this team had all three things working for them throughout the tournament and down the stretch, they finally understood that their defense could make the difference. They really could win it all.

Mark McMillin, a close family friend, is another character-legacy example. Mark was a good man. Our families grew up together in the married housing complex at

Ferris State University, while I was going to graduate school at Central Michigan and working part-time.

We did everything together—we camped and canoed, played sports, attended events, and reveled in each other's company whenever we could. Our families were knit together in close kinship over years of relationship building.

Like me, Mark had recently retired and spent most of his time enjoying his family, working part-time, and playing golf, the game he so passionately loved, at the Lynx Golf Course in his hometown of Otsego, Michigan.

Sadly, in June of 2018, Mark passed away suddenly. I made plans to attend his funeral along with Bernadette and my daughter Seena. But when we got there, it wasn't a funeral at all; it was a celebration. Almost an entire town came out to commemorate and honor a man who had served his whole community. The legacy he left took my breath away, not to mention the profoundly touching effect he had on his wife, children, and grandchildren.

One of his granddaughters, Ryann Gilchrist, wrote a beautiful obituary. She titled it, "The Pond of Remembrance," which summed up his character and love for those around him, especially his family and everyone he touched. If I could have just a measure of the influence, he had on all those he served during his lifetime, I would be an overly blessed man. What a character legacy one single human being has left.

Strangely enough, on the same day I received the news of Mark's passing, I got phone calls about two other close friends, who also passed away within hours of Mark's death.

Carole "Mother" Vaughn, who worked for Nike and set up the trips for college basketball coaches and their wives, as well as baseball and football trips that were also sponsored by Nike. Mother Vaughn left a remarkable character legacy that will resonate in the hearts of many coaches, their wives, and Nike employees for decades to come. Bernadette and I have gone on these Nike trips for over twenty years and we were close to her and loved her.

A paraphrase of a famous quote that reflects the impression Mother Vaughn left on all those whose lives she touched is this, "*People may forget what you say to them, people may also forget what you do for them, but people will never forget how you made them feel.*" God bless Mother Vaughn! She made everyone feel loved, appreciated, and worthy.

The other friend who left the earth that day was C.M. Newton, a special human being. He was the Naismith Memorial Hall of Fame honoree, athletic director at University of Kentucky, and Hall of Fame coach at Vanderbilt University. Later in his career, he was instrumental in helping the NIT formulate an operational structure that has flourished over the years. He helped me receive a lower seed in the tournament as a mid-major recipient numerous-times. He was not afraid of helping the little man, even in the higher position he held.

I respected C.M. deeply because of the character he demonstrated throughout his administration and life. C.M. left a character legacy that many have followed, especially his son, Martin Newton, who is presently the athletic director at Samford University.

Leaving a legacy is not merely about the successes people will remember when you're gone, it's about the values you instill and the paradigm that you pass on.

> *Leaving a legacy goes beyond just leaving mere success, it creates a lasting impression over those who wish to keep you and your memory alive.*

Success is predicated on what one has accomplished, but leaving a legacy starts with you and continues once you're gone, touching everyone along the way. A character legacy has an even greater impact on those you touch, because

Waters Family Hall of Fame Induction

to them you will never be forgotten, your life becomes a treasured history which they can study and pattern their own lives after, being all the better for it.

But by far, the most important character legacy a man can leave is the one he confers to his children and grandchildren, since they are the ones who can breathe new life into a vision he started, but didn't have a chance to finish. They will likely have the most intimate knowledge of what their father or grandfather wanted to be remembered for, what was most important to him, thus, they can keep their legacy thriving.

But even for those without wives or children, or who have estranged families, all is not lost. Coaches especially, are mentors and paternal figures, and have an exceptional opportunity to enrich someone else's existence in life and in their death, by leaving a worthwhile legacy for them to replicate.

Gary and Sean Waters
Legacy Portrait

King David said to his people, "One generation shall praise Your works to another..." (Psalm 145:4)

Start creating a legacy of your own today that will allow others to not only enjoy the fruits of your labor, but also reflect on your memory with admiration, inspired by your life's work.

CONCLUSION
THE NEED FOR CHARACTER COACHES

Sports do not build character. They reveal it.
—**Heywood Broun**, American Journalist, Sportswriter, Newspaper Columnist, and Editor (New York City)

T he profession is in dire need of coaches of character. Joe Ehrman once said:

"One of the great myths in America is that sports build character. They can, and they should. Indeed, sports may be the perfect venue in which to build character. But sports don't build character unless a coach possesses character and intentionally teaches it."

As coaches, we favor certain principles and ideologies over others, ones that we promote, embody, and reinforce what we believe about what's best for teams we lead. These beliefs stem from either moral standards or some other form of criteria we've received and internalized, which we ultimately shape into our own guiding criteria.

It's up to us as coaches, to carefully distill our attitudes, beliefs, and values, make sure they align with integrity and character, the touchstones of a worthwhile program. We must establish our own philosophies through the lenses of our own experiences and experimentation, then build them around the character traits we want to exemplify.

It's up to us as coaches, to carefully distill our attitudes, beliefs, and values to make sure they align with integrity and character, the touchstones of a worthwhile program.

For this reason, if your coaching philosophy is rooted in character principles, then your values and character should align with the principles identified throughout this reading.

I coached for over forty-three years and during that time I was committed to being an example of a character coach to the coaches and players I had under my supervision.

In addition, I've tried to provide my coaches and players with whatever they needed to reach their goals and potential. When a player and his parents see a coach putting God first in his life, demonstrating honesty and integrity in the things he does, he's epitomizing what it is to be a character coach.

The principles and insights I've shared in this book could well serve as a starting point for any coach who wants to breathe new life into his team culture, create a manifesto for his staff to use as a signpost in their decision-making, or present his players with a fresh vision.

I know it's lofty, but my hope and prayer are that I've laid out my case for character in ways that coaches, parents, and players can relate to, that my stories resonate, and that if the things I've covered weren't important before, they are now.

These concepts aren't widely promoted in the society we live in today. Though I try to never succumb to the temptation, I recognize the allure of certain worldly gains that can provide short-term gratification, but cost something far more precious in the long run.

Regardless of the profession, sports, business, or entertainment, character-building is important to prepare each person for the rigors of life.

In my early years of coaching at both Eastern Michigan University and Kent State University, I had to immediately establish my own character example in each program.

At Eastern Michigan, I was the associate head coach, so I had to get approval from head coach Ben Braun to create an environment where character development and value clarification were the standard. Without Ben's buy-in and example, it would have been hard to establish this culture.

*Ben Braun receiving award from The State
Legislature in Lansing, Michigan*

The early '90s teams at Eastern Michigan were successful. In my last year at EMU we advanced to the NCAA Sweet Sixteen of the tournament. We lost to the University of North Carolina, coached by the late Dean Smith in that Sweet Sixteen match. Dean was the ultimate character coach.

Later, when I became a Division 1 head coach, I had the opportunity to witness this firsthand, not only while Dean Smith coached, but also off the court. Dean and I spent quality moments together during the Nike trips I mentioned earlier. The wisdom he shared with me during those trips was priceless and helped me grow throughout my character development journey.

Another thing worth mentioning about Dean was his love for minority advancement in the profession. He was the first coach to integrate the basketball program at the University of North Carolina, as well as one of the earlier coaches to do it in the Atlantic Coast Conference (ACC). Dean stood for everything I respected about being a coach of character.

My first head coaching position, I was hired by Laing Kennedy the athletic director at Kent State University. Laing was one of the best human beings and administrators that I have ever been associated with.

Laing selected me as the eleventh head coach at Kent State because he was impressed with my character and integrity first. Truthfully, that's all he could base his decision on since he had little to go on in the way of my head coaching experience. He took a chance on me and it paid off because I possessed character, and so did he.

Establishing a culture of character and integrity at Kent State was vital in creating its development and success. We achieved a great deal of success at KSU during those years, two conference championships, two NCAA Tournament appearances, and one NIT post-season tournament quarter finals appearance over a five-year period.

Being the head coach, it was my responsibility to set the tone from the very beginning. I had to be the example because everyone in the program was following my lead. I knew the example I provided was important to the coaches, as well as the players, because most people tend to emulate the example of the leader they are following. You know the saying…*so goes the leader.*

But what was more important to me was seeing my coaching staff commit their lives to integrity and embrace character-building everyday as examples for our players.

Since college basketball has gone under some scrutiny in recent times, it's now more important than ever for coaches to focus on how they should carry themselves, since they are representatives of the sport.

The best way for them to represent the profession is through their character, a quality they can easily control. John Wooden once said about coaches, "Be more concerned with your character than your reputation, because your character is what you are, while your reputation is merely what others think you are."

The principles you have read about in this book are designed to strengthen your commitment to being a character-driven coach. If this is your desire, then as with

Coach Waters making history at Cleveland State
(Courtesy of Cleveland State University)

anything else, merely reading about the principles is not enough—you must put them into action. Daily action!

This means you must not only talk the talk; you must walk the walk as well. Character coaching is a lifestyle and a journey for the committed, but it is also a rewarding and profitable one. In fact, I'm sure you've often heard it said before, but it bears repeating: the journey *is* the reward. So, live it, treasure it, enjoy it, Character Coach!

ACKNOWLEDGMENTS

I genuinely believe that the creation of any masterpiece is the result of the design and influence of the efforts of more than the one it's credited to. This truth applies when acknowledging those who help you formulate the thoughts you put on paper.

There were several people who had a great impact on the completion of this book, and for that I am eternally grateful. However, I must acknowledge a special group of people who stood out in their support to make sure that this book was designed to reach those who are truly interested.

Since I was venturing into unknown territory, identifying these people became an important undertaking. My wife, Bernadette was the first to help me with the recording, writing and typing of the initial manuscript. I am so very thankful to have her as the love of my life and her unwavering support in this endeavor.

Next, I need to thank Jennifer Wainwright, for her steadfast commitment to the editing, proofreading, organizing, as well as the modification of this accurate and finished product. I must further thank Shannon Wainwright, for his consultation and assistance on the initial formulation of the book.

In addition, I must thank Greg Murphy, my Sports Information Director at Cleveland State, for his work in compiling the statistical data, current photos and the accurate information, which helped substantiate the story behind this book.

I would also like to acknowledge Larry DeSimpelare, a longtime assistant and lifelong friend, for his amazing memory and recollection of past events, people, and experiences. Larry, you really helped me remember so many dates and names I had forgotten.

Furthermore, I must thank my sister-n-law Bernadine Walker, for her unwavering commitment in helping me formulate and structure the pictures throughout the book.

To Raoul Davis and his staff at Ascendant Group, thank you for your tireless effort in the creation and development of my brand, and for the securement of a book endorsement to further cement my reputation in the literary industry.

To David Hancock and his team at the Morgan James Publishing company, thank you for your support and for doing such an exemplary job in helping me to navigate the nuances of the publishing process.

The work that each of you devoted to this book is commendable and worth more recognition than a simple thank you. I am eternally and sincerely grateful for the roles you've played in allowing my dream to become a reality.

Finally, I would be remiss if I did not acknowledge and honor the Lord of my life, Jesus Christ, who I put first in everything I do, and who brings to light the work that each person added to the completion of this incredible book.

ABOUT THE AUTHOR

 Gary Waters has achieved an impressive amount of accomplishments during his 40-plus seasons in college basketball. In his 21 years as a head coach—five at Kent State, five at Rutgers and 11 at Cleveland State, Waters amassed 365 wins and led 12 of his 21 teams to the postseason tournaments.

One of the most respected coaches in the collegiate game by his peers, Waters served as a coach for the USA Basketball Men's National Team Trials at the U.S. Olympic Training Center and coached the USA Junior World Championship qualifying team.

Waters has been elected to three Hall of Fames. He was inducted into Ferris State Athletic Hall of Fame in 2002 and was enshrined into the Kent State Varsity "K" Hall of Fame in 2006. He was also inaugurated in the city of Detroit High School Hall of Fame in September of 2019.

In addition, he has received several national awards, earning the John Lotz "Barnabas" Award by the Fellowship of Christian Athletes 2010, and the 2015 Master Coach Award from the Nations of Coaches. He was a finalist for the 2014 and 2015 Ben Jobe Award, which is presented annually to the top minority coach in college basketball. At the end of Waters final year before retirement, Waters received the President's Medal Award from Cleveland State, the first time a non-facility member was honored.

Waters is a member of the National Association of Basketball Coaches (NABC), where he served as a member of the NABC Board of Directors, as well as serving on the NABC Ad Hoc Committee of the NCAA Men's Basketball Tournament Selection.

Waters became head coach at Kent State in 1996, leading the Golden Flashes to a 92-60 record in five seasons (1996-01). He was one of only three coaches in the Mid-American Conference history to earn MAC Coach of the Year honors in successive seasons (1999 & 2000).

Waters moved on to Rutgers University for the 2001-02 season and quickly made an impression. He led Rutgers to the National Invitational Tournament in first season. For

Waters' achievements, he was honored as Coach of the Years from the Metropolitan Writers Association of New York.

Waters returned to Northeast Ohio in 2006 when he was named the head coach at Cleveland State University. Over next 11 years he guided the Vikings to 194 wins the most by a head coach in program history.

During Waters 11-year tenure at Cleveland State, all seniors who completed their eligible in the program earned their degree under Coach Waters. The program also earned recognition from the NCAA four times for having a program in the top-10 percent of the Academic Progress Rate (APR) among all Division 1 basketball programs (2012, 2013, 2014 & 2015).

A native of Detroit, Michigan, Waters was an all-city and all-state performer at Detroit Mackenzie High School. Waters went on to received honorable mention All-American, as well as, all-conference and all-region at Oakland Community College (1969-71). He transferred to Ferris State in 1972, becoming a first team all-league performer and all-district selection. Waters was selected by the Detroit Piston to participate in the NBA draft trials (1974). He was later in that year drafted by Spain to play in the international league.

Waters earned his bachelor's degree from Ferris State in Business Administration in 1975, a few years later he earned a second bachelor's degree in Business Education in 1978. The year following his first bachelor's degree, Waters obtained his master's degree in Educational Administration from Central Michigan in 1976.

Gary is married to his high school sweetheart, Bernadette and they have two children, Sean and Seena Allen, and seven grandchildren. They are both retired and reside in Tampa, Florida.